BLEST PAIR OF SIRENS

(AT A SOLEMN MU

BLEST pair of Sirens, pledges of Heav'n's joy,

Sphere-born, harmonious sisters, Voice and Verse,

Wed your divine sounds, and mixt power employ,

Dead things with inbreathed sense able to pierce.

And to our high-raised phantasy present

That undisturbèd song of pure concent,

Aye sung before the sapphire-coloured throne

To Him that sits thereon,

With saintly shout and solemn jubilee;

Where the bright Seraphim, in burning row,

Their loud, uplifted angel-trumpets blow,

And the Cherubic host, in thousand quires,

Touch their immortal harps of golden wires,

With those just spirits that wear victorious palms,

Hymns devout and holy psalms

Singing everlastingly.

That we on earth with undiscording voice

May rightly answer that melodious noise;

As once we did, till disproportioned sin

Jarred against nature's chime, and with harsh din

Broke the fair music that all creatures made

To their great Lord, whose love their motion swayed

In perfect diapason, whilst they stood

In first obedience, and their state of good.

O may we soon again renew that song,

And keep in tune with Heav'n, till God ere long

To His celestial concert us unite,

To live with Him, and sing in endless morn of light.

JOHN MILTON

Blest pair of Sirens
AN ODE

Words by Milton

Music by C. Hubert H. Parry
Arr. by C. S. Lang

That we on earth with un-dis-cord-ing voice

That we on earth with un-dis-cord-ing voice

That we on earth with un-dis-cord-ing voice

That we on earth with un-dis-cord-ing voice

May right-ly an-swer that me-lo - dious noise; As once we

May right-ly an-swer that me-lo - dious noise; As once we

May right-ly an-swer that me-lo - dious noise; As

May right-ly an-swer that me - lo - dious noise; As once

CHORUS-SOPRANO
Allegro

O may we soon a-gain re-new that song, And keep in tune with

Heaven, and keep in tune with Heaven, till God ere long To His ce-

O may we soon a-gain re-

O

-les-tial con-cert us u-nite, And keep in tune with Heaven,

-new that song, And keep in tune with Heaven, and keep in tune with

may we soon re-new that song, And keep in

13

CHORAL WORKS FOR MIXED VOICES

BACH
CHRISTMAS ORATORIO
For soprano, alto, tenor & bass soli, SATB & orchestra

MASS IN B MINOR
For two sopranos, alto, tenor & bass soli, SSATB & orchestra

ST MATTHEW PASSION
For soprano, alto, tenor & bass soli, SATB & orchestra

BRAHMS
REQUIEM
For soprano & baritone soli, SATB & orchestra

ELGAR
GIVE UNTO THE LORD PSALM 29
For SATB & organ or orchestra

FAURE
ed Desmond Ratcliffe
REQUIEM
For soprano & baritone soli, SATB & orchestra

HANDEL
ed Watkins Shaw
MESSIAH
For soprano, alto, tenor & bass soli, SATB & orchestra

HAYDN
CREATION
For soprano, tenor & bass soli, SATB & orchestra

IMPERIAL 'NELSON' MASS
For soprano, alto, tenor & bass soli, SATB & orchestra

MARIA THERESA MASS
For soprano, alto, tenor & bass soli, SATB & orchestra

MASS IN TIME OF WAR 'PAUKENMESSE'
For soprano, alto, tenor & bass soli,i SATB & orchestra

MONTEVERDI
ed Denis Stevens & John Steele
BEATUS VIR
For soloists, double choir, organ & orchestra

ed John Steele
MAGNIFICAT
For SSATB chorus, instruments & organ

ed Denis Stevens
VESPERS
For soloists, double choir, organ & orchestra

MOZART
REQUIEM MASS
For soprano, alto, tenor & bass soli, SATB & orchestra

SCARLATTI
ed John Steele
DIXIT DOMINUS